# THE AGE OF
# DINOSAURS

written by Sarah Albee
reviewed by Robert E. Budliger

Reader's
Digest
Children's Books®

Pleasantville, New York • Montréal, Québec • Bath, United Kingdom

# Studying Dinosaurs

Dinosaurs were ancient reptiles that lived on earth for about 165 million years. But about 65 million years ago, all the dinosaurs that lived here mysteriously died off. Today, all we have left of them are some **fossils** of bones, footprints, and other bits and pieces.

When most people think about dinosaurs, they imagine huge, ferocious creatures. But not all dinosaurs were huge. And not all of them were scary. Some types of dinosaurs had beaks, some had feathers, and others had horns. Some lived alone, and some lived in herds of a thousand or more. In fact, one of the most amazing things about these animals is how very different they were from one another. So far, modern scientists have discovered and named more than 800 different types of dinosaurs—but new types are being found all the time.

## When and Where

The history of the earth is divided into eras, and the eras are then divided into periods of time. The **Mesozoic** era—known as the Age of Dinosaurs—is divided into three periods: the **Triassic,** the **Jurassic,** and the **Cretaceous.** Today we live in the Quaternary period of the Cenozoic era. Humans have been on earth for about 4 million years. Compare that to the dinosaurs' 165 million years!

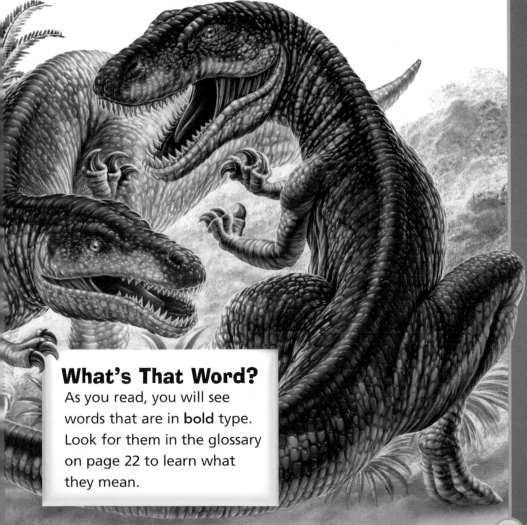

## What's in a Name?

Although the word *dinosaur* means "terrible lizard," dinosaurs were not lizards! Like lizards and other modern reptiles (alligators, crocodiles, turtles), dinosaurs laid eggs. But unlike modern reptiles, dinosaurs walked with their legs directly under their bodies, not splayed out at their sides.

## What's That Word?

As you read, you will see words that are in **bold** type. Look for them in the glossary on page 22 to learn what they mean.

# The Age of Dinosaurs

**DINOSAUR DIET KEY**
- Meat-eater
- Plant-eater

*Kannemeyeria*

*Scaphognathus,*
pterosaur

• *Eoraptor*

• *Plateosaurus*

• *Dilophosaurus*

• *Allosaurus*

PREHISTORIC TIMES

PALEOZOIC ERA

550 million years ago

# PERIOD

# CRETACEOUS PERIOD

Euoplocephalus

Stegosaurus

Deinonychus

Mamenchisaurus

Barosaurus

Lambeosaurus

Tyrannosaurus rex

Triceratops

| TRIASSIC | JURASSIC | CRETACEOUS | | |
|---|---|---|---|---|
| MESOZOIC ERA | | | | CENOZOIC ERA |

248 million years ago    206 million years ago    144 million years ago    65 million years ago    Today

# Life in the Triassic

When dinosaurs first appeared, the earth was one enormous landmass surrounded by water. Dense forests, filled with ferns, palmlike plants, and cone-bearing trees, grew near the coastlines. There were no flowers anywhere, and most of the land was a hot, dry desert.

Nearly all of the animals lived near the coast, where it was easier to find food and water. Reptiles and huge fish hunted in the ocean. More reptiles—ancestors of the earliest dinosaurs—hunted on land. Spiders, scorpions, centipedes, and insects scuttled among the plants and desert sands. Many kinds of animals had evolved and disappeared by the time the Triassic came to an end. But not the dinosaurs. They survived and thrived. And they gave rise to new kinds of dinosaurs, which eventually spread all over the earth.

## Look Out Below!

The first dinosaurs shared the earth with the first crocodiles, tortoises, and rat-size mammals. Up in the air swooped flying reptiles, known as **pterosaurs.** Pterosaurs such as *Pterodactylus* and *Pteranodon* were relatives of dinosaurs.

During the Late Triassic a Plateosaurus *might have grazed on some ferns alongside meat-eating* Coelophysis. *The meat-eaters were probably more interested in eating small lizards than in attacking the huge plant-eater.*

# Jurassic Giants

Some of the biggest animals ever to walk on land appeared during the Jurassic period. The plant-eating **sauropods** were among these. Sauropods had thick feet and legs, similar to those of a present-day elephant. They had long necks that allowed them to browse in the treetops, or to sweep their heads from side to side to graze on ground plants. Their peglike teeth ripped off leaves, which were then crushed in an organ called the gizzard. Their huge size helped them scare off most **predators**. Some sauropods probably fought off enemies by cracking their whiplike tails. They may also have traveled in herds.

By the Jurassic, many meat-eating dinosaurs had evolved into even larger animals. *Allosaurus* was one of the biggest, standing as tall as an elephant. Like modern wolves, *Allosaurus* probably hunted in packs and went after large **prey**.

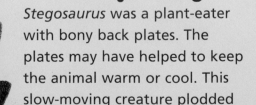

## Pokey Pacing

*Stegosaurus* was a plant-eater with bony back plates. The plates may have helped to keep the animal warm or cool. This slow-moving creature plodded along like an armored tank.

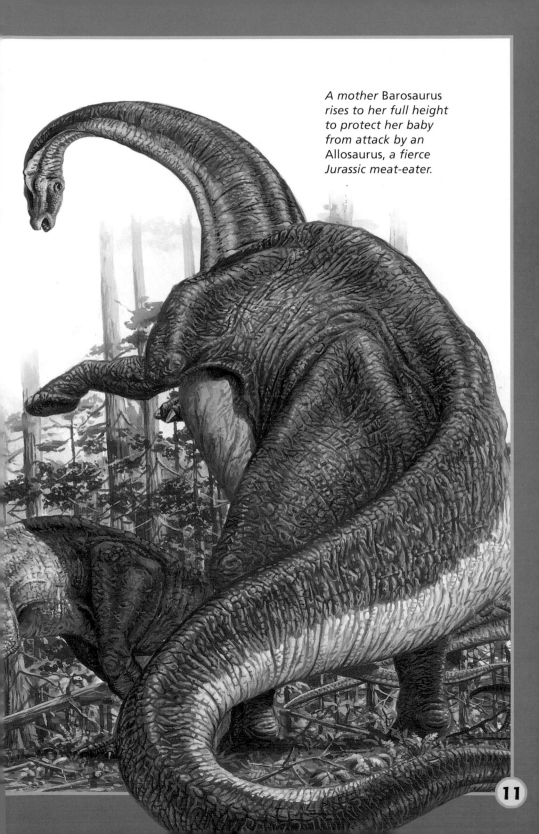

*A mother* Barosaurus *rises to her full height to protect her baby from attack by an* Allosaurus, *a fierce Jurassic meat-eater.*

# Cretaceous Creatures

Over a long period of time, many types of dinosaurs, such as *Allosaurus* and *Stegosaurus*, gradually disappeared. But during the Cretaceous period other kinds of dinosaurs developed to take their place.

One of these groups was the **tyrannosaurids**. The best known of this group, *Tyrannosaurus rex*, ruled what we now think of as the North American continent in the Late Cretaceous. This meat-eater walked on two legs and grew to be 40 feet long. Its terrifying jaws flashed about 60 sharp teeth.

Plenty of smaller but equally fierce meat-eaters thrived during this time, too. These creatures had large brains for their small size. Many of them hunted in packs.

*Many plant-eating dinosaurs adapted special features for defense. The heavy bone at the end of the Ankylosaurus's tail formed a club that could do serious damage, even to an attacking Tyrannosaurus.*

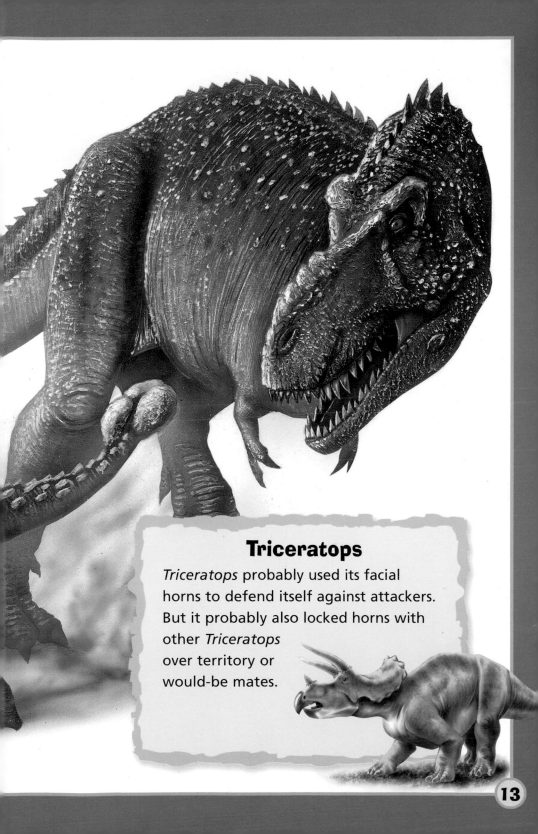

## Triceratops

*Triceratops* probably used its facial horns to defend itself against attackers. But it probably also locked horns with other *Triceratops* over territory or would-be mates.

# The Dinosaurs Disappear

This much we know: About 65 million years ago a giant space rock—a comet or an asteroid—slammed into the earth with incredible force. The rock was so huge and landed with such force that it left a crater more than 100 miles wide in what is now the Yucatan Peninsula of Mexico.

Many scientists believe that the impact created firestorms that filled the air with soot and smoke for many years, causing the eventual disappearance of many plants and animals, including dinosaurs. This massive die-off of so many living things is known as the **Cretaceous extinction**. It is the most widely held theory to explain the disappearance of dinosaurs. But there are other theories, too: continuous volcanic eruptions and rapid climate changes. We will probably never know the exact cause with certainty.

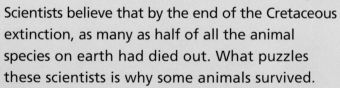

## Just Dumb Luck?

Scientists believe that by the end of the Cretaceous extinction, as many as half of all the animal species on earth had died out. What puzzles these scientists is why some animals survived. Why did the dinosaurs and flying reptiles die off, while crocodiles, turtles, lizards, birds, and ancient mammals survived?

# Other Extinction Theories

The world's climate became too cold, and dinosaurs froze or starved to death.

The world's climate became too hot for dinosaurs to survive.

Volcanic eruptions poisoned the air and the land.

# Fossil Clues

Everything we know about dinosaurs has been carefully chipped out of rocks and dirt all around the world by scientists called **paleontologists**. But there is still so much we don't know. New discoveries about dinosaurs are being made all the time.

In fact, very few dinosaurs left fossil remains. The conditions had to be just right for an ancient animal to leave any evidence of its existence. It had to die in a place where its body would be quickly covered by sand, mud, or water. When that happened, usually only the hard parts of the animal (bones and teeth) became fossilized. But sometimes the soft parts of an ancient animal (skin, scales, feathers, even droppings) left imprints in the surrounding rock. These softer parts hint at what these ancient animals looked like, what they ate, and how they moved. And by studying their fossilized nests and eggs, we can even learn something about how dinosaurs took care of their babies.

## Foot Finds

Fossilized footprints reveal fascinating information. Scientists use them to estimate a dinosaur's weight and even its speed. Footprints can also tell us about the behavior of an entire dinosaur herd. In some herds the bigger animals moved in front and along the sides, protecting the smaller ones on the inside from predators.

# How a Fossil Is Formed

1. A dinosaur body washes into a river. Soon only the bones remain.

2. The skeleton is buried under sand or mud. Over thousands of years, the bones are replaced by minerals, forming fossils as hard as stone.

3. Movements inside the earth bring the fossilized bones back up to the surface. **Erosion** uncovers the bones, and people discover them.

# Dino Discoveries

Long before anyone knew about the existence of dinosaurs, people were finding fossils of dinosaur bones. People in ancient times thought they were the bones of dragons or giants. It was not until the early 1800s that scientists began to figure out what sort of creatures possessed these bones.

Re-creating a dinosaur skeleton from bones and fragments is not an easy job. It's like putting together a giant jigsaw puzzle without being able to look at the picture on the box! A lot of guesswork is involved.

## No Such Thing as a Brontosaurus!

Back in 1879 paleontologist Othniel Marsh believed he had discovered a new sauropod dinosaur. He named it *Brontosaurus.* The skeleton he unearthed was nearly complete except that it was missing a skull, feet, and bits of its tail. The bones were reconstructed for display in a museum, and a head from a different skeleton was put on the body that Marsh had uncovered. But scientists recently realized that the fossils used to reconstruct *Brontosaurus* had come from more than one kind of dinosaur—the body Marsh had found was that of *Apatosaurus,* and the head was from *Camarasaurus*. For 100 years the dinosaur had been wearing the wrong head!

At first scientists believed dinosaurs looked like big lizards with sprawling legs. By the end of the 1800s, they realized that dinosaurs stood upright on their legs, like horses and birds.

There is still so much we don't know about dinosaurs. Why did some dinosaurs have feathers? What kinds of sounds did they make? Dinosaur discoveries are still making headlines today, even 65 million years after the creatures became extinct.

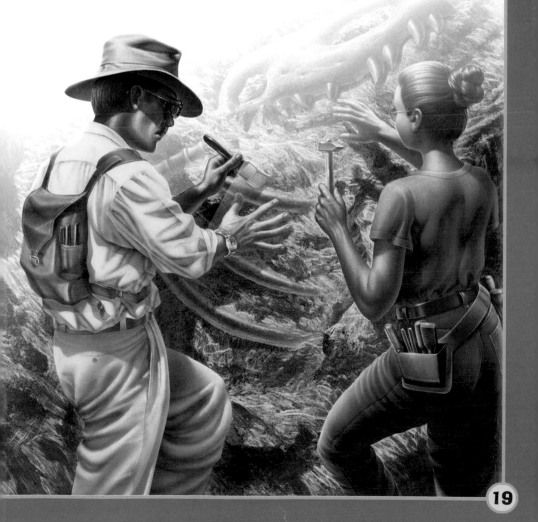

# Dino Descendants

Are birds the descendants of dinosaurs? This theory is gaining acceptance by many paleontologists. Birds today don't look much like their dinosaur ancestors, but they do share many physical similarities: a wishbone, swiveling wrists, and three forward-pointing toes on each foot.

Recently scientists discovered that dinosaurs had a breathing system that was very similar to that of birds—and like birds, many dinosaurs had light bones. Alligators and crocodiles are also probable relatives of dinosaurs, but they are not quite so closely related as birds.

## Lucky Break

In 2003 a team of paleontologists discovered a massive *Tyrannosaurus* bone. They were forced to saw the bone in half in order to load it onto a helicopter. From the bone's core, tiny bits of brown tissue fell out. When these bits were tested, scientists learned that the animal had been dead for 68 million years and that the tissue resembled that of a chicken. This evidence further supports the theory that birds are related to dinos.

# The Hips Matter

Scientists divide all types of dinosaurs into two main groups according to the shape of the dinosaur's hip bones. The **saurischians** had hips shaped like those of a lizard (top), and the **ornithischians** had hips shaped like those of a bird (bottom). All the meat-eaters belonged to the lizard-hipped group, as did a few of the plant-eaters. All the other plant-eaters were bird-hipped.

# Glossary

**Cretaceous:** A period of time that began about 145 million years ago and ended about 65 million years ago

**Cretaceous extinction:** The massive die-off of the dinosaurs at the end of the Cretaceous period

**erosion:** The wearing away of the surface of the earth by the action of water, wind, or glacial ice

**fossils:** The remains or imprints of an ancient living thing found in rocks or stony soil

**Jurassic:** A period of time that began about 205 million years ago and ended about 145 million years ago

**Mesozoic:** The Age of Dinosaurs era, which began about 245 million years ago and ended about 65 million years ago

**ornithischians:** Bird-hipped dinosaurs that ate plants; one of the two orders of dinosaurs

**paleontologists:** Scientists who study ancient plants and animals

**predators:** Animals that hunt other animals for food

**prey:** Animals that are hunted by other animals for food

**pterosaurs:** Flying reptiles that evolved during the Late Triassic period

**saurischians:** Lizard-hipped dinosaurs, primarily meat-eaters but some plant-eaters and some that ate both meat and plants; one of the two orders of dinosaurs

**sauropods:** A group of giant plant-eating lizard-hipped dinosaurs that existed from the Late Triassic to the end of the Cretaceous; included some of the largest animals known

**Triassic:** A period of time that began about 248 million years ago and ended about 205 million years ago

**tyrannosaurids:** A group of the largest meat-eating dinosaurs that ruled the earth during the Cretaceous